# Two Nations, One Land

## The Mexican-American War

Book on American Wars Grade 5 | Children's Military Books

**BABY PROFESSOR**
EDUCATION KIDS

First Edition, 2021

Published in the United States by Speedy Publishing LLC, 40 E Main Street, Newark, Delaware 19711 USA.

© 2021 Baby Professor Books, an imprint of Speedy Publishing LLC

Baby Professor Books are available at special discounts when purchased in bulk for industrial and sales-promotional use. For details contact our Special Sales Team at Speedy Publishing LLC, 40 E Main Street, Newark, Delaware 19711 USA. Telephone (888) 248-4521 Fax: (210) 519-4043.

1 0 9 8 7 6 * 5 4 3 2 1

Print Edition: 9781541960435
Digital Edition: 9781541963436
Hardcover Edition: 9781541984813

See the world in pictures. Build your knowledge in style.
www.speedypublishing.com

# Table of contents

THE UNITED STATES AND MEXICO FOUGHT IN THE MEXICAN-AMERICAN WAR.

**H**ave you ever fallen out with a friend? This does happen from time to time. People do not always see eye to eye. A lot of friends manage to patch things up. They go on to form strong friendships. The governments of different countries also have disagreements. They do not always solve them peacefully. Sometimes they go to war. This happened between the United States and Mexico.

The United States and Mexico fought in the Mexican-American War. This book will give the background to the war. It will talk about some things that happened during the war. The results of the war will also be mentioned.

6

# Chapter One:
# Background to the Mexican-American War

**A** part of what led to the United States and Mexico to go to war had to do with some of the history of Texas.

CADDO INDIAN VILLAGE

JUMANO INDIANS

COMANCHE INDIANS

## A Brief Look at the History of Texas:

The first people to ever inhabit Texas were Native American Indians. They occupied the area for <u>millennia</u>. There were different tribes to do so. Three tribes were the Caddo, Jumano, and the Comanche.

9

During the 1500s and 1600s, explorers from Spain and France arrived. The Spanish built some settlements there.

The meaning of the word *Texas* is *allies* or *friends*. It comes from a Native American Indian language. In the Spanish language, it is spelled Texas. In 1821, Mexico gained control of the area. The area was then named Tejas.

DURING THE 1500S AND 1600S, EXPLORERS FROM SPAIN AND FRANCE ARRIVED.

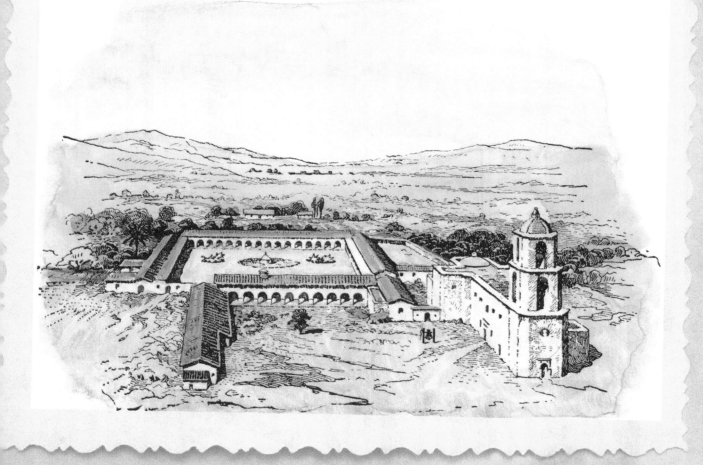

TYPICAL ARRANGEMENT OF A COLONIAL SPANISH MISSION SETTLEMENT IN TEXAS.

THE AMERICANS SETTLED IN TEXAS AND MADE IT THEIR HOME.

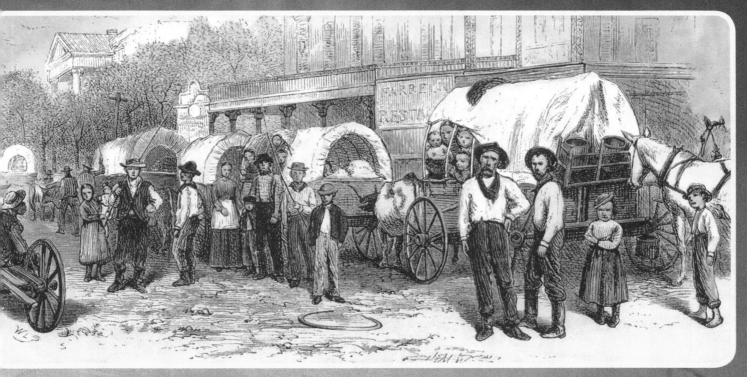

WAGON TRAIN OF SETTLERS LEAVING FOR TEXAS.

After Texas came under Mexican rule, Americans were asked to move to Texas. Many would arrive. They settled there and made it their home. It was not too long before there would be problems. Neither the American newcomers nor the Mexicans could see eye to eye.

IN 1835, TEXANS REVOLTED AGAINST THE MEXICAN GOVERNMENT.

In 1835, Texans revolted against the Mexican government. Americans in Texas fought to become independent from Mexico. There were battles between both these groups.

In 1836, Texas would get its independence. It became known as the Lone Star State. It still has this nickname.

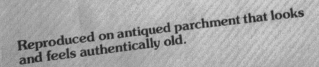

UNANIMOUS

# DECLARATION OF INDEPENDENCE,

BY THE

## DELEGATES OF THE PEOPLE OF TEXAS,

IN GENERAL CONVENTION,

AT THE TOWN OF WASHINGTON,

WHEN a
tect the liver
people, from
derived, and
happiness it w
being a guara
inalienable rig
the hands of e
When the Fed
of their country
support, no lo
tence, and the
ernment has bee
their con-ent, fr
Republic, compa
a consolidated (
in which every
that of the army
the eternal enem
ready minions of
struments of tyra

Texas Declaration of Independence
March 2, 1836

Reproduced on antiqued parchment that looks and feels authentically old.

SOUVENIR REPRODUCTION OF THE TEXAS DECLARATION OF INDEPENDENCE IN 1836.

Texas would remain a republic for almost ten years. In 1845, Congress agreed that Texas could join the United States. This was known as the <u>annexation</u> of Texas. A year would not pass before the United States and Mexico went to war. There were two main reasons for this war. They both had to do with quarrels over land.

TEXAS STATE FLAG WAVING OVER ALAMO, SAN ANTONIO, AFTER BEING ADMITTED TO THE UNION.

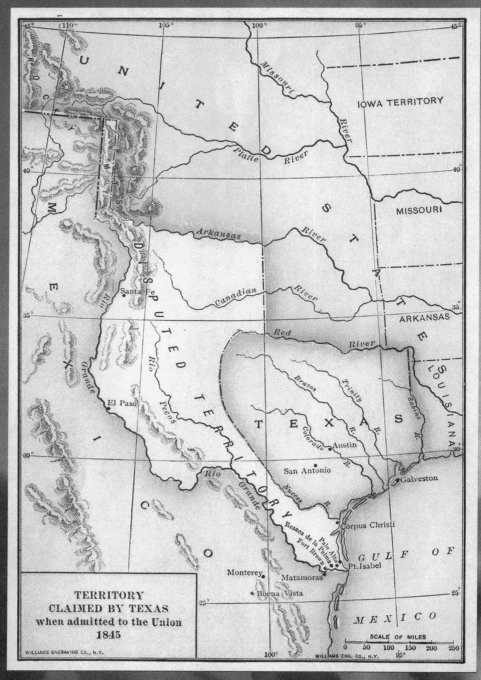

MAP OF THE TERRITORY CLAIMED BY THE REPUBLIC
OF TEXAS WHEN ADMITTED TO THE US IN 1845.

18

## Land Disputes Between the United States and Mexico:

The United States and Mexico disputed land in two different locations. One dispute involved the exact point where Texas ended, and Mexico began. To the American government, Texas extended south to the Rio Grande. To the Mexican government, Texas stopped further north. This would be at the Nueces River. Since Texas had once belonged to Mexico, the Mexicans felt that they were correct about the land border. The Texans had fought for the land, so they equally felt entitled to set the borders.

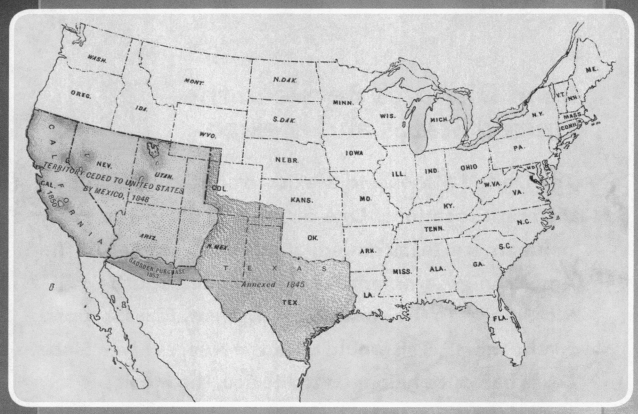

THE U.S. WANTED LAND THAT IS NOW NEW
MEXICO, ARIZONA, AND CALIFORNIA.

The second dispute had to do with an offer to buy land. The United States government wanted to buy more land from Mexico. The United States wanted land that is now New Mexico, Arizona, and California. The problem is that Mexico did not want to sell any of it.

The American President at the time was James Polk. He had a strong desire to buy this land. Polk was <u>fueled</u> by his firm belief in an idea called the Manifest Destiny. This idea had two main beliefs. One was that the United States had the right to land that lay between the Atlantic and the Pacific Ocean. The second was that the Americans were <u>destined</u> for it. The belief was that God had given the United States this right.

JAMES POLK

The term the Manifest Destiny was first published in 1845. An editor by the name of John O'Sullivan came up with it. He included it in an essay. He said it when he was talking about Texas. He believed that Texas should be allowed to join the Union. The term Manifest Destiny became well used after this essay was published.

JOHN O'SULLIVAN

AN ALLEGORICAL FEMALE FIGURE OF AMERICA, POTENTIALLY
AN ANGEL, LEADING PIONEERS WESTWARD.

PRESIDENT POLK DID HIS BEST TO TRY TO PERSUADE
MEXICO TO TAKE MONEY FOR THE LAND.

Polk did his best to try to persuade Mexico
to take money for the land. Mexico remained
firm in its decision against it. It had never truly
accepted the fact that it had lost Texas to the
United States. This would remain a tense issue
for the Mexicans.

In his efforts to change their minds, Polk got a group of men together. He then sent them to Mexico to enter talks. The Mexican government would not even meet them. Relations became so bad that the Mexican government refused to even talk to the American government. The Mexican government would not even talk to people in Texas. Relations were cut!

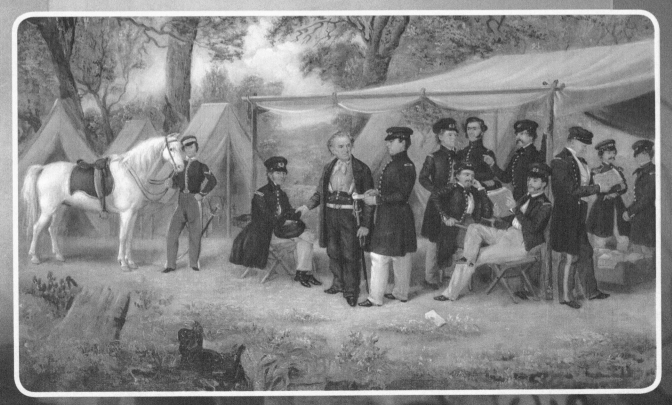

POLK GOT A GROUP OF MEN TOGETHER AND THEN SENT THEM TO MEXICO TO ENTER TALKS.

After Polk realized that he was not going to persuade the Mexicans to sell land, he decided to invade. He went to Congress and received approval to go to war with Mexico. This was in May 1846.

PRESIDENT POLK WENT TO CONGRESS AND RECEIVED APPROVAL TO GO TO WAR WITH MEXICO.

US ARMY APPROACHING MEXICO CITY DURING THE MEXICAN-AMERICAN WAR.

# Chapter Two:
# Battles and Events of the Mexican-American War

Although Polk had been preparing for war, it was the Mexican government that made the first move. Mexican troops were sent across the Rio Grande. They marched ahead and attacked the American soldiers there.

MEXICAN TROOPS ON THE MARCH DURING THE MEXICAN–AMERICAN WAR.

Several battles would follow. It did not take Polk long to send in his troops. Both sides would see victories and losses. Thousands of soldiers would lose their lives. Some died in battle while others lost their lives to diseases.

THE BATTLE OF PALO ALTO WAS THE FIRST MAJOR BATTLE OF THE MEXICAN-AMERICAN WAR FOUGHT ON MAY 8, 1846, ON DISPUTED GROUND FIVE MILES FROM THE MODERN-DAY CITY OF BROWNSVILLE, TEXAS.

The United States attacked Mexico from a few different points. The United States Army had a general by the name of Zachary Taylor. He already had experience helping to defend Texas. This was when the Texans were revolting against Mexican rule.

GENERAL ZACHARY TAYLOR

Taylor and his men went to the Texan border to face Mexican soldiers there. His men would end up winning a couple battles against the Mexican troops.

TAYLOR AND HIS MEN WENT TO THE TEXAN BORDER TO FACE MEXICAN SOLDIERS THERE.

MEXICAN ARTILLERY CAPTURED BY GENERAL ZACHARY TAYLOR AT THE
BATTLE OF MONTEREY IN THE MEXICAN-AMERICAN WAR, 1846.

Once the Mexican-American War started, Taylor was an obvious choice to lead soldiers in it. Taylor led troops across the Rio Grande. He and his troops would go on to win different battles. They took control of Monterrey, a Mexican city.

GENERAL ZACHARY TAYLOR ATTACKING MONTEREY, MEXICO DURING THE MEXICAN-AMERICAN WAR, 1846.

In a later battle, Taylor's troops would defeat the Mexicans again. This happened in the Battle of Buena Vista. Taylor and his men were victorious even though they were outnumbered. Taylor would be remembered as a hero.

BATTLE OF BUENA VISTA

GENERAL ZACHARY TAYLOR AT
THE BATTLE OF BUENA VISTA,

CHARGE OF MEXICAN LANCERS AGAINST US FORCES AT
BUENA VISTA DURING THE MEXICAN-AMERICAN WAR.

GENERAL WINFIELD SCOTT
MAKING A TRIUMPHAL
ENTRY INTO MEXICO CITY
ON A WHITE CHARGER.

GENERAL WINFIELD SCOTT LEADS US FORCES INTO
MEXICO CITY TO END THE MEXICAN-AMERICAN WAR.

Another general, Winfield Scott would be remembered for taking over Mexico City. This was an important capture because it was the capital city of Mexico.

GENERAL WINFIELD SCOTT

Other areas of land that are now parts of the United States were also captured. One of them was New Mexico. It was taken by troops led by Stephen Kearny. Kearny was a colonel in the U.S. Army.

STEPHEN KEARNY

STEPHEN KEARNY CAPTURING SANTA FE, NEW MEXICO ON AUGUST 18, 1846, DURING THE MEXICAN-AMERICAN WAR.

Kearny, along with two others, would go on to take California. The other men were John Charles Frémont and Robert F. Stockton.

JOHN CHARLES FREMONT

ROBERT F. STOCKTON

Frémont knew the area well. He had traveled the West before and helped to make maps of the area. He served as Lieutenant Colonel in the Mexican-American War. Stockton's rank was as Commodore.

FREMONT HAD TRAVELED THE WEST BEFORE AND HELPED TO MAKE MAPS OF THE AREA.

John Charles Frémont had a big influence in the history of California. He was a governor through the military governorship. He would become one of the first people to be elected as a senator there. There is a mountain peak in this state that was named in his honor. It is Fremont Peak.

FREMONT PEAK IN CALIFORNIA.

ANTONIO LOPEZ DE SANTA ANNA

SANTA ANNA ALSO SERVED IN THE MEXICAN ARMY AS AN OFFICER.

One of the men who led Mexico into battles was Antonio López de Santa Anna. He served as the President of Mexico. He was elected to this office in 1833. He was known for being more like a dictator than an elected official. Santa Anna also served in the Mexican Army as an officer.

FLIGHT OF SANTA ANNA ON A MULE AT THE BATTLE OF CERRO GORDO ON APRIL 17, 1847, DURING THE MEXICAN-AMERICAN WAR.

From the time Santa Anna was first elected president, Mexico would have different leaders. This went on for about twenty years. Power would change hands many times. Santa Anna would be in charge ten different times during this period! While he was in charge, he led Mexican soldiers against American soldiers in the Mexican-American War. After losing a few battles to the American soldiers, the Mexicans made him leave Mexico. He would return later.

# The Treaty of Guadalupe Hidalgo:

The Mexican-American War officially ended when both governments signed a treaty. The treaty was called the Treaty of Guadalupe Hidalgo. Representatives from the government of both countries signed it on May 2, 1848.

COVER OF THE EXCHANGE COPY OF THE TREATY OF GUADALUPE HIDALGO.

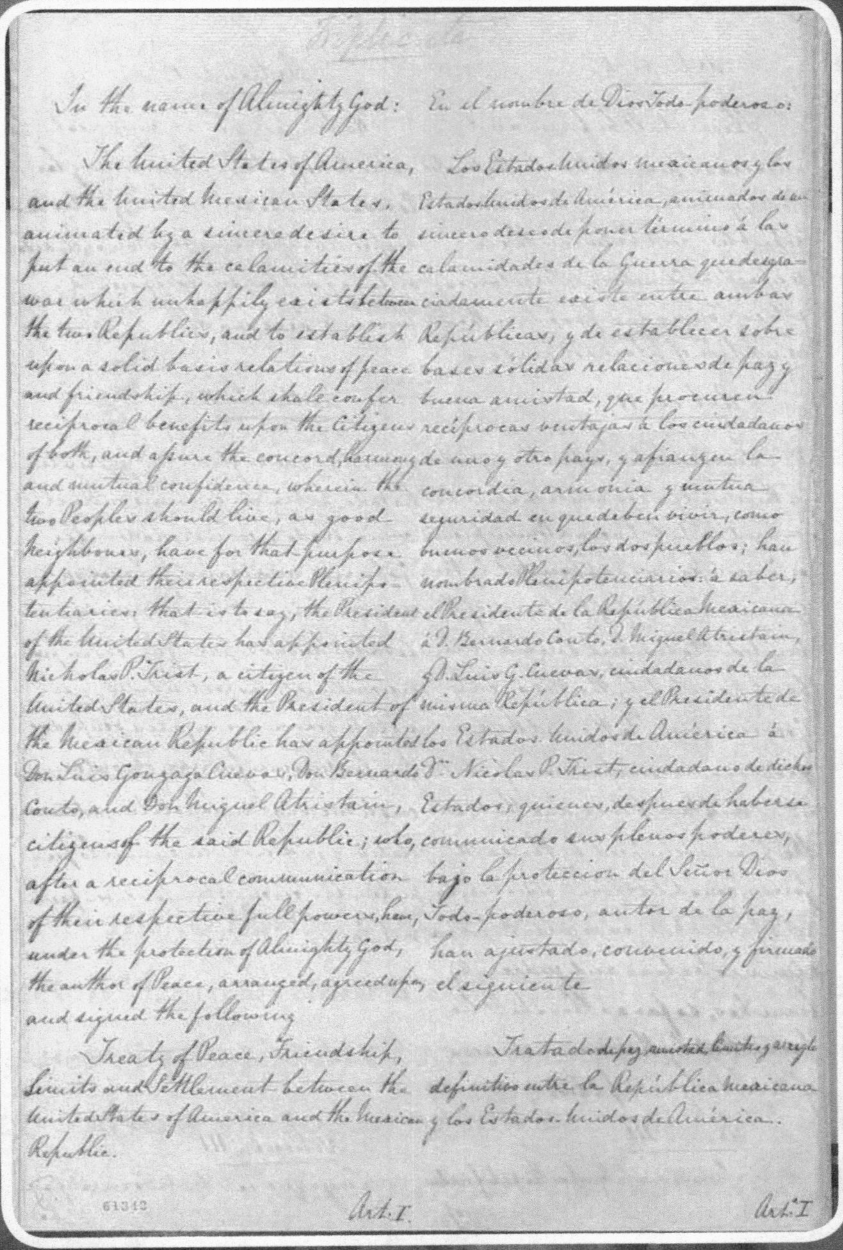

In the name of Almighty God:

The United States of America, and the United Mexican States, animated by a sincere desire to put an end to the calamities of the war which unhappily exists between the two Republics, and to establish upon a solid basis relations of peace and friendship, which shall confer reciprocal benefits upon the citizens of both, and assure the concord, harmony and mutual confidence, wherein the two Peoples should live, as good Neighbours, have for that purpose appointed their respective Plenipotentiaries: that is to say, the President of the United States has appointed Nicholas P. Trist, a citizen of the United States, and the President of the Mexican Republic has appointed Don Luis Gonzaga Cuevas, Don Bernardo Couto, and Don Miguel Atristain, citizens of the said Republic; who, after a reciprocal communication of their respective full powers, have, under the protection of Almighty God, the author of Peace, arranged, agreed upon, and signed the following

Treaty of Peace, Friendship, Limits and Settlement between the United States of America and the Mexican Republic.

Art. I

En el nombre de Dios Todo-poderoso:

Los Estados Unidos Mexicanos y los Estados Unidos de América, animados de un sincero deseo de poner término á las calamidades de la Guerra que desgraciadamente existe entre ambas Repúblicas, y de establecer sobre bases sólidas relaciones de paz y buena amistad, que procuren recíprocas ventajas á los ciudadanos de uno y otro pays, y afianzen la concordia, armonía y mutua seguridad en que deben vivir, como buenos vecinos, los dos pueblos; han nombrado Plenipotenciarios: á saber, el Presidente de la República Mexicana á D. Bernardo Couto, D. Miguel Atristain, y D. Luis G. Cuevas, ciudadanos de la misma República; y el Presidente de los Estados Unidos de América á D. Nicolas P. Trist, ciudadano de dichos Estados; quienes, despues de haberse communicado sus plenos poderes, bajo la proteccion del Señor Dios Todo-poderoso, autor de la paz, han ajustado, convenido, y firmado el siguiente

Tratado de paz, amistad, límites y arreglo definitivo entre la República Mexicana y los Estados Unidos de América.

Art. I

61343

FIRST PAGE OF THE ORIGINAL TREATY.

NICHOLAS TRIST

The person who signed it on behalf of the United States government was a man named Nicholas Trist. Trist had been sent to Mexico by President Polk. The purpose was to negotiate a peace deal with the Mexican government.

TREATY OF GUADALUPE HIDALGO SIGNED BY TRIST.

Apparently, the president thought that Trist was taking too much time. He sent word for Trist to return so that somebody else could be sent. Trist did not heed the request. Instead, he remained in Mexico. While there, he and the Mexican government signed the treaty into effect.

# Chapter Three:
# Results of the Mexican-American War

The terms of the Treaty of Guadalupe Hidalgo would give both countries something. The terms gave the United States a lot of land. The terms favored Mexico with money.

THE TERMS OF THE TREATY OF GUADALUPE HIDALGO
GAVE THE U.S. LAND AND MEXICO WITH MONEY.

# Land and Money:

The United States would receive a large area of land. The total added up to more than 500,000 square miles or 1.3 million square kilometers. It started to the west of the Rio Grande. It ended at the Pacific Ocean. All had belonged to Mexico. The land that the United States received would become different states. They were Texas, Utah, New Mexico, California, Nevada, the west part of Colorado and Arizona.

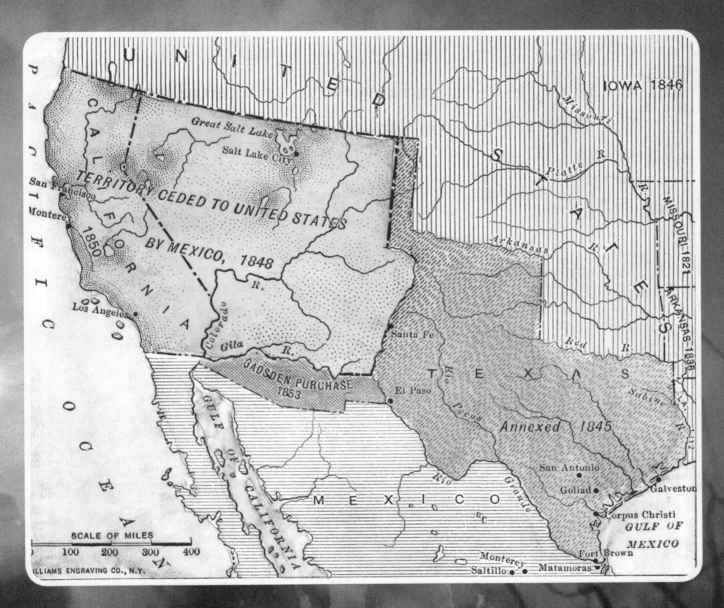

MAP OF THE TERRITORY CEDED BY MEXICO TO THE U.S.

While Mexico lost a lot of land, it gained a lot of money. The United States government had to pay the Mexican government fifteen million dollars. This was in exchange for the land.

THE U.S. GOVERNMENT HAD TO PAY THE MEXICAN
GOVERNMENT FIFTEEN MILLION DOLLARS.

GENERAL ZACHARY TAYLOR WOULD
BE HONORED AS A WAR HERO.

General Zachary Taylor would be honored as a war hero. He was elected as the next president of the United States.

## Did you know?

Zachary Taylor was elected to the presidential office in 1848. He became the twelfth person to be elected to this role. He would only remain in office for sixteen months.

He died on July 9, 1850. Most of his adult life was spent in the U.S. military. He served in the military for forty years.

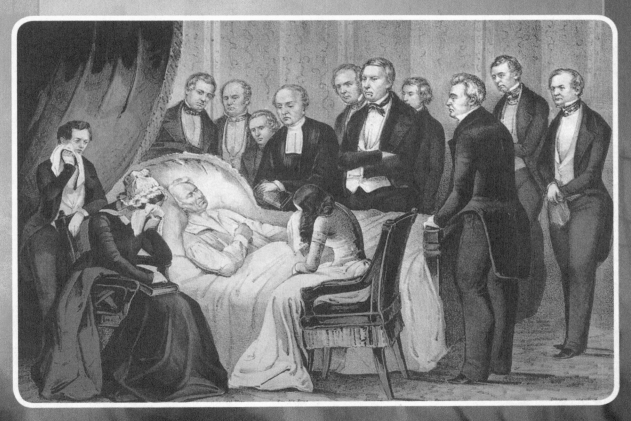

THE DEATH OF ZACHARY TAYLOR

# Debates Over Slavery:

Now that the war was over, the new president and Congress would have to deal with slavery. Slavery was a big issue.

There were new states in the country. What happened is that there would be different rules for different states. Texas had been given permission to keep slaves when it joined. California, on the other hand, was permitted to ban the practice. Some other states were given the right to choose for themselves. They could vote on the issue at a state level.

THE DEBATE OVER SLAVERY WOULD NOT GO AWAY.

This did not prove to be a good solution. The debate over slavery would not go away. There would have to be an official ruling on it.

THE AMERICAN CIVIL WAR WOULD BEGIN IN 1861.

There would be another result of the Mexican-American War. The United States would end up having a civil war. In other words, American states would be fighting against each other! The American Civil War would begin in 1861. One factor that would lead to it was slavery. The nation would be divided from north to south on this issue.

# Summary

The United States and Mexico went to war against each other. The war started in 1846 and lasted for two years. It was fought over disputes about land. At the time, many people in the United States, including the President, believed in the Manifest Destiny. This was an idea that the United States should get all the land from the east coast to the west coast of North America.

Many soldiers lost their lives in the war. The Treaty of Guadalupe Hidalgo officially brought it to an end. The United States got a lot of land. Mexico got a lot of money from the United States in return. Both countries would end up going to war with themselves. For more information about American history, look for more Baby Professor books!

# Glossary

**Millennia (pg. 9):** thousands of years

**Annexation (pg. 16):** One country or group of people taking land from another country or group of people

**Fueled (pg. 21):** In this context, fueled means influenced by a strong feeling

**Destined (pg. 21):** Something that happened because it was said that it would happen

Made in the USA
Monee, IL
22 November 2024

70918296R00044